WHAT TO DO WHEN YOU DON'T HAVE A BOOK COMING OUT

WRITER CHAPS

SHORT BOOKS FULL OF OUTSTANDING ADVICE FROM AUSTRALIA'S TOP SPECULATIVE FICTION WRITERS

Season One

You Are Not Your Writing and Other Sage Advice, Angela Slatter

From Baby Brain To Writer Brain: Writing Through A World of Parenting Distractions, Tansy Rayner Roberts

Eyes on the Stars: Writing Science Fiction & Fantasy, Sean Williams

The Martial Art of Writing and Other Essays, Alan Baxter

Capturing Ghosts on the Page, Kaaron Warren

Headstrong Girl: How To Live A Writer's Life, Kim Wilkins

Season Two

What To Do When You Don't Have A Book Coming Out & Even More Sage Advice, Angela Slatter

WHAT TO DO WHEN YOU DON'T HAVE A BOOK COMING OUT

& Even More Sage Advice

ANGELA SLATTER

Brain Jar Press
PO Box 6687
Upper Mt Gravatt, QLD, 4122
Australia
www.BrainJarPress.com

Copyright © 2022 by Angela Slatter

The moral right of Angela Slatter to be identified as the author of this work has been asserted.

All rights reserved. No part of this book may be reproduced in any form or by any electronic or mechanical means, including information storage and retrieval systems, without written permission from the author, except for the use of brief quotations in a book review.

Cover design by Peter Ball
Cover Image: *Woman at home with a cat working and resting. Pop art retro; retro comic blue background;* studiostoks /Shutterstock.

ISBN: 978-1-922479-25-9 (Ebook) | 978-1-922479-26-6 (Chapbook)

Contents

Ten Things You Need to Know About Grants	1
On Reading	10
Top 5 Networking Tips for Writers	13
On the Importance of Being Edited (and Editing)	19
What to Do When You Don't Have a Book Coming Out	27
How Long Does Stuff Take?	34
Finding an Agent: the Ugly Truth	38

Ten Things You Need to Know About Grants

I've been fortunate enough to be awarded some grants during my career (by Arts Queensland, the Copyright Agency and the Australia Council for the Arts). To balance things out, I have also **not** received many of the grants for which I've applied. As I am a writer, I'll be specifically directing this guide towards getting grants for literature, but there's enough general advice in here for anyone in the Arts to walk away with some useful information. I'm also Australian, so this applies specifically to the Australian system of public Arts funding (d'uh). As with anything in your writing career, be a responsible self-directed author, and do your own research to fill in the blanks. That's the whole point of Google.

So, here are ten things you need to know about grants[1]:

1) Many Hear the Call But Few Are Chosen

Grants.

Everyone wants one.

Everyone thinks they deserve one.

Everyone's chances of getting one are very low indeed.

The sad fact is that there's a limited pool of Arts funding to go around. Artists don't tend to attract sponsorships the way sportsfolk do ... and I think that's a shame, because honestly, who'd be better than writers for advertising coffee, booze and yoga pants? Well, maybe not the yoga pants so much, lycra is very unforgiving and we're not always given to activities involving movement or sweat.

My point? Have realistic expectations. What stage are you at in your career? What will you get out of this project? What will you produce? Is your project going to look like a good investment of public funds? I know that doesn't sound very artistic or creative, but government funding bodies need to justify their expenditure. They need to be able to see some sort of return on investment, whether that be a new work written (although preferably written **and** published) or a skills development course undertaken to get you to the next level of your creative career.

2) Your Application Will Take A Few Weeks

That's not the decision-making process (that will take months) — that's the time it will take for you to prepare and pull your application together. You're going to need to discuss, in a considered and articulate fashion, the scope and aims of your project, how you're going to do The Thing, and what you'll get out of it (production of a new work, career development, skills acquisition and development, market and audience development, etc).

You might need to ask for support letters from people with standing in the writing/publishing industry/community who know your work. These people need to be prepared to commit to paper that they believe you will (a) benefit from the grant, (b) will make the most of the opportunity, and (c) will move forward in your career as a result. Hint: do not ask them the night before, it's the equivalent of telling your mum you need an asparagus costume for school the very next day.

If you're applying for a grant to produce a new novel, you will also need to provide writing samples to show the grant body the standard of your work — so, not the micro-fiction you threw down one Saturday night after not much thought, but rather a lot of cheap wine. An already published piece is generally better than an unpublished piece (it shows a publication track record), and a piece that has won an award or had multiple reprintings is better again (again, showing some kind of achievement in your field helps). You might be required to submit a sample of the new work you're hoping to get a grant to create, so make sure you polish it until it shines. A well-crafted short example is better than a weak overly long extract.

The upshot of all this is: be prepared. It will take time to write, edit and proof your application (because a document filled with grammatical infelicities and spelling eccentricities is not going to help your cause). And again — I cannot emphasise this enough — it will take anyone who agrees to provide a support letter time to phrase that correctly, so don't ask for these things at the last minute. They don't get written quickly or easily. A good letter of support will not only mention your writing ability but also help to demonstrate how your proposed project will move you forward. Respect everyone's time.

3) Don't Put All Your Eggs In One Basket

There are several organisations to which you can apply for grants, **but** you cannot rely on getting one from any of them.

If you're applying for a big grant to buy yourself time away from other forms of paid employment to write a novel/cycle of poems/short story collection, then **do not** plan on getting that grant. Don't plan on that being your only source of income, with no safety net. If you do assume you'll get it, trust me when I tell you that you are going to be devastated **if**/when it doesn't come to fruition. I learned that the hard way, so you don't have to:

never have only one plan. Nowadays, my back-up plans have back-up plans.

So: what is your Plan B if you don't get your grant? It needs to be more detailed than just throwing yourself on the fainting couch and howling for a couple of days whilst living on nothing but whiskey and Pringles.

How are you going to keep writing? How are you going to complete this project whether you get a grant or not? Because that's another thing a funding body will want to see: that you are going to do this project come hell or high water, grant or no. That you're committed to your artistic career.

That you will commit art no matter what.

You will need to make sure that you prepare a realistic budget for your project. Check with the organisation to see what level of detail they will require for the grant budget (and also for the acquittal process at the end, if you need to keep receipts, etc). If you're applying for a travel grant to go to do a course somewhere, make sure your budget takes in all the costs, then show what proportion you're paying and what proportion you're proposing a grant will cover.

A travel grant will mean airfares, course registration, ground transfers, accommodation, travel insurance, incidentals (like phone costs, printing costs), a per diem rate for meals (you can use the government travel rate charts for public servants as a guide — once again, Google is your friend), etc. A grant to take a significant period off other paid employment to produce a significant piece of literature will need to budget for your expenses during that time: rent/mortgage payments, health insurance, food and utilities bills, associated travel costs for research trips, and more. Again: you will need to figure out what portion is going to be met by you, and what portion is going to be covered by one or more grants.

Grant bodies are also going to want to know that you're (a) not expecting them to fund 100% of your project, (b) that you've applied to other grant bodies to help bear the cost, and (c) that you've got other forms of income to put towards the project yourself.

Keep in mind that there are also fully funded fellowships and residencies out there that you can apply for. They should pay you a living stipend for the period of the fellowship or residency, and if they're located overseas, you'll often get your airfare paid for as well by the administering body. The Aerogramme Writers' Studio maintains a very useful list of such opportunities on their website (again: not exhaustive, so do your own further research).

4) It Takes Persistence

You might not get the first grant you apply for. You might not get the second, or third, or tenth. But: keep doing what you're doing. A grant body will note if you keep applying, they will note if you've kept doing your art in spite of everything, kept achieving. But there is no point in throwing a hissy fit because you didn't get the grant you applied for, no point in flouncing off declaring you're never applying again — who is that supposed to teach a lesson to?

It's also particularly unwise to throw public hissy fits at or in the direction of the funding body. Or even private hissy fits directed at the employees of that body. Why? If only because you might one day decide to apply for another grant — do you really want someone to remember you and say "Oh, hells no."

Persist in a polite but bloody-minded fashion. Show a pattern of persistence, show a pattern of determination and application. Who knows? Maybe one day you'll get a grant coz someone ends up feeling sorry for you. Pity is also a tool.

5) It's Not All About You

The point of this is: what are you going to give back to your community?

If you **do** get this grant to help you advance your career, what are you going to do to put something back or pay something forward? If you teach writing, or mentor newer writers, then that's your first means of transmitting useful info. Tell your classes about what you learned. If you made connections and new networks as part of your project, then share that information with your students who are likely to be newbies with not a lot of clues. Help them learn how the systems work (because grants for newbies are very rare indeed). You can't make someone into a decent kind generous human being, but you can at least be an example of how one functions. Being a good example of a generous networker is the least you can do. Like, literally.

Similarly, if you've got an online presence, then write an article about your experience and what you learned (hey, just like this chapbook is distilling and sharing what I've learnt! Will you look at that?). Document the advantages and pitfalls. It's not all about the successes either, so if you encountered problems that others might also find, then talk about them — I'm not saying have a whinge-fest, but just let folk know there were stumbling blocks.

And if you get a publication outcome of out this project, then make sure you acknowledge the help of the funding organisation on your website and in the front matter of your book. Achievements like that are important outcomes for the grant bodies and help keep them getting funded, so **we** keep getting funded.

6) You Need To Acquit

If you do get a grant, then at the end of your project you will need to acquit it to the satisfaction of the funding body. This means you need to show that you spent the public funds you were given in the manner you promised — i.e., did not spend it in dive bars or on online shoe shopping binges.

That might take the form of keeping receipts, letters, or

certificates of completion, or simply writing a report that shows you achieved the goals set out in your original application. If there were things you were unable to do, then document that as well and give reasons as to why not. If you did something over-and-above the stated goals, then document that as well (international publication, optioning of film rights to the book, etc), and reiterate the places where you will acknowledge the assistance of the grant organisation.

7) Be Realistic About What You're Going to Do

There's no point in applying for funding for a project that's so jam-packed that you've actually got no realistic hope of achieving everything. The people assessing grant applications will have a good idea of what is and is not achievable in a particular amount of time. You need to find that fine balance between doing too much and too little, between a realistic workload (because a project **is** work) and throwing everything into the soup.

8) If You Change It, You Need Approval

If you do get a grant, but the parameters of your project change *before* you start it (e.g. part of your professional development or one of your appearances falls through), then you need to alert the granting body as soon as possible. It might change the amount you get, but if you can undertake replacement activities, you should be fine. Just make sure you supply confirmation of the new activities, like enrolment or invitation to participate details. It's better to catch this at the start rather than having to justify it after you return.

9) Remember That You Might Never Get One

I hate to be a Debbie Downer on this and remind you of points 1 and 3, but it is a sad fact for which you need to be prepared. Don't rely on getting a grant. Ever. Like awards, this is a crap shoot, a gamble, buying a lottery ticket. However, the advantage is that if you keep applying you show persistence, and you will (hopefully) get better at writing grant applications. Plus, you will build up a suite of grant applications that you can adapt from one round to the next so you're not always reinventing the wheel.

10) Don't Be An Asshole

Someone else got a grant and you didn't? That's life. Not everything comes with fries. Don't whine or bitch, don't complain, don't tell others that your project was better. Don't be an asshole.

Your project might simply not have held up against a range of others. Perhaps you didn't adequately demonstrate how it would help your career, or there wasn't enough clear benefit to the Arts community, or it simply wasn't an appropriate fit (hint: if you're at uni and you applied for an Arts grant in order to complete part of your post-graduate degree, then that won't fly because there's post-grad funding for that within your uni). Just be gracious; congratulate those folk who get a grant this round. Maybe even ask them about their application — maybe they'll be good eggs and let you see it, so you can take notes for your next attempt. They might even end up being people who'll be willing to write you a support letter later on.

No matter what happens, just try to be a decent human being.

In Conclusion

This isn't everything you need to know. These are just the highlights that have occurred to my tired brain. Do your own research, and remember that your local writers' centre should also maintain a list of funding bodies. Some of them might even list upcoming opportunities in a weekly or monthly bulletin. Remember that there are websites to visit, but that you should also make a point to chat (yes, on the phone) with the lovely folk at the funding body just to get a better feel for what they're looking for, if there are specific things they won't fund, etc.

Essentially, if you only take away two things from this article, let them be (a) persist and (b) don't be an asshole.

Some Funding Bodies Of Interest

- Arts Queensland (each state in Australia has some similar body, so do the Google).
- The Australia Council for the Arts
- The Copyright Council's Cultural Fund
- The Neilma Sidney Literary Travel Fund

---

1. Not an exhaustive list.

On Reading

Specifically, on the reading you need to do when you're a writer.
Reading out loud.
In front of an audience.
This is terrifying enough on its own, but you can manage it. Here are a few hints that I find useful:

1. Practise your reading **before** you turn up at the place of the reading.
2. Practise it more than once. More than twice. Go up to five times (after that you'll freak yourself out).
3. Time it — the average reading should go for between 3-5 minutes coz that's generally all the attention span the audience can bear (unless you're an awesome storyteller who can hold people's hearts and minds and ears in the palm of your hand).
4. Be aware that what's written on the page, what looks wondrous to the eye, is not necessarily going to do the tongue and ears any favours. When you read aloud in the privacy of your own lounge room, bedroom, kitchen, gazebo, panic room, listen carefully. Are you breathless? More so than nerves can explain? Then

that lovely long sentence you slaved over needs to be read differently. Cut in two or three, pauses added so you can breathe, and the listener can enjoy your words. That huge passage of description? Do you really need it all? Is some of that already covered by other lines, and you were just making a point in print? Cut it back, or out entirely (NB: be careful not to take out a salient point or something that gives the story meaning.)

5. This is an entirely personal choice, but my rule is: don't drink before you read. You might think it soothes your nerves, coats your tongue with silver, but a nervous person tends to be a gulper and before you know it, you've had two or three, your cheeks are red and you're laughing uncontrollably, falling over your own feet and impaling yourself on the mic stand (if you're in luck — then you can be carted off to hospital and avoid the reading). Trust me, no one will talk about the awesome reading.

To illustrate the flensing technique, I've included a page of the story I read at Muse in Canberra in 2017 before Conflux started. Kaaron Warren, Ellen Datlow and I all went along and chatted to a full house about *Alice in Wonderful*, and Ellen's new anthology *Mad Hatters and March Hares*, in which Kaaron and I both have stories. You can see what I took out and what I left in on the next page.

hugging safety of a burrow and there's an earthy smell, too, that almost reminds him of home.

Safe.

Safe'ish.

Not so safe that he doesn't keep glancing at the door whenever it opens. Not so safe that he doesn't already know he can exit quickly through the back office, the kitchen, the tiny men's room, and even tinier Ladies. He knows what to look for in newcomers.

When he'd come through—and come through properly this time, not just jumping over the border then back again like a child on a dare ~~or defying a parent who'd said *This far and no further*~~—he'd changed. Changed his shape to become like one of the humans. However, he wasn't entirely *solid*, not entirely three-dimensional, but flimsy, weightless as a playing card, feeling as if he turned side-on he might disappear. Not that the humans noticed, ~~as such a subtlety was beyond their blunt perceptions~~—but he knew this strange flatness, lightness, thinness afflicted the Queen's assassins, too. He could pick the bounty hunters from the way they moved, as if fearful a strong wind would carry them away.

'Another?' The barman's voice startles Rabbit, but he does his best not to show it; he smiles at the young man who wears a plain black shirt and matching jeans, no nametag for this is a not a place where names matter. He's handsome in a rough sort of fashion; a good bath and some styling and he'd pass for civilised. Just the sort Rabbit used to like, over on the other side, although he finds he prefers the women here.

'Yes, please,' says Rabbit softly, wistfully, 'same again.'

~~The barman has large hands, black hairs curl across the backs of his fingers; Rabbit imagines it's on his chest, too, a densely tangled inverted triangle, and thinks of the line of it that will surely travel from his belly button down to the loins. Not very muscular, slender, with ropey veins in his forearms that remind him of the Ace.~~

~~Oh, but he's melancholy tonight! Perhaps he should slow down on the whiskey. Perhaps not.~~

Rabbit watches the barman surreptitiously at first, then realises the youth isn't interested, doesn't care if he's sized up or not; isn't the sort to take offence at being found attractive by another man.

Top 5 Networking Tips for Writers

Well for starters, "networking" isn't a dirty word. Unfortunately, sometimes it feels dirty. Some writers will tell you that the entire idea of networking dilutes or sullies your art – that you should get back to starving in your garret, producing a masterpiece that people will magically know about when it's done. The word has most certainly received a bad rap courtesy of all those movies about high finance, serial killers, and people who compare the size of their business cards. But it needn't be a word to set you all aquiver in a bad way. Let's reframe it as a useful word, a helpful word, a word that doesn't make you think of some wanker in an expensive suit ahead of you in the queue ordering a half-caf vanilla mocha frappuccino with a light sprinkling of lemongrass. So, here are five ideas to get you thinking differently about networking and to help you to identify networking opportunities.

1) Learn To Play Nice With The Other Kids And Share Your Toys

One of the worst examples of writerly behaviour I've seen over the years is 'hoarding', i.e. not sharing market information or submission opportunities with others. It's selfish behaviour based on the flawed idea that there's a limited opportunity pool for writers, so the fewer people who know about an open call for submissions, the smaller amount of competition there will be, and therefore you've got a better chance of being accepted. Here's the thing: if your work is good enough, it will rise to the top of the slush pile, and it won't matter how many other submissions are lurking there.

If you know of a market, share it around. Especially if you're not a good fit for it – why would you keep that information to yourself? What good will that do anyone? Similarly, even if you know of a market you are a good fit for, don't be a dog in a manger. Be generous, share the information. Someone else who has some success from a tip you passed on might just remember you kindly when they have a useful piece of intel.

2) Not All Facets Of Writing Are Solitary

Just as it takes a village to raise a child, so it takes a lot of people to raise a writer. Often those people are beer and winemakers, but there are also others who are not entirely booze-related. Writing groups – okay, those are often booze-related – fulfil a valuable series of functions, which may include but are not exclusive to, the following:

- Contact with others is important as it reminds you how to speak and interact with someone other than the cat. Sometimes it even gets you out of the house to a place where you can exchange money for goods and services such as cupcakes and the making of coffee. This is good.
- Critiquing of your work by others, which can help you see problems you've been blind to as well as finding ways to fix said problems. One of my favourite maxims is that you can't proofread your own work – I mean, you can, but you're probably going to suck at it

no matter how good a writer you are, because you know what you meant to write, so oftentimes you'll see it there (even when it's missing or there's a typo, or you've played fast and loose with sentence construction). So, outside eyes on your work is also good.
- A writers' group is a great place to do that whole sharing of your toys thing. Getting leads on agents and publishers with open submission periods, anthologies that are looking for work, and/or – and this one is very important – those "writer beware" moments when you can learn which publisher doesn't pay on time (or at all). Which editor, while terribly enthusiastic, cannot actually spell or place an apostrophe to save their life? Or which "agent" wants to charge you a reading fee? (Hint: NONE of them should).
- Given that many of us are fairly antisocial and socially challenged, we can get very nervous at the idea of talking to people we don't know. Personally, I break out in a rash and babble, big babbler, me – but this is where the writers' group can be perfect. You can nominate some of your group time for "practice runs": talking to people, role playing (with or without costumes, as you prefer). Just running through a series of small talk and questions can sometimes help make the whole idea of "networking" a little less daunting.

3) Find People Who Know More Than You And Learn From Them

As a writer, you need to be ever vigilant against the idea that you'll reach a point where you know everything – you don't and you won't. There's *always* something to learn, or something you might have forgotten and need to remember. There's something to be picked up from everyone you ever meet, even if that something is "Don't behave like a complete pillock." Where can you find such fonts of knowledge? Writers' centres, conventions, conferences, institutions of higher learning with good, practical writing programs, and writers' festivals. Some writers' centres run publishers & agents seminars, where you can go along and listen to a panel of publishers and agents (funnily enough) talk about what they're looking for and how best to approach them.

As with all of life's experiences, some behavioural hints can be helpful:

- When you work up the courage to talk to someone at a seminar or con or what-have-you, don't monopolise them, especially if they're the special guest at an event, or someone on the last leg of a long book tour. Like good readings, this sort of interaction should be no longer than five minutes long (unless you get on famously, in which case, buy them a drink). Exchange pleasantries, ask your most pressing question, then depart gracefully and graciously. Say "thank you".
- If you feel you've made a connection with someone, then offer a business card or contact details, but for the love of all that's holy or otherwise, don't be insistent. Shrieking "Please read and critique and give to your publisher my sixteen volumes of zombie-vampire-Star Wars slash fiction" is not likely to get you the result you want. Remember that people in the industry talk; they talk to each other, they compare notes. Don't be the nutter or the rude person that everyone knows about.
- If you find yourself foundering, or indeed floundering, then give a cheery "Well, I must be moving on", and abort, abort, abort! But do not be disheartened, don't decide you're never talking to an Important Person ever again. Perfecting the art of networking, of talking

to people, takes time. Go back to your writers' group and do a few more role plays. Don't give up.
- I cannot emphasise this enough: be grateful and gracious. Even if the person you've spoken to has behaved like the proverbial pillock, don't stoop to their level. Remain polite and dignified. You can always get revenge later when you've had time to think up something really good. Joking!

4) Build Mutually Beneficial Relationships

This is the core of good networking. What this means is that networking isn't all about you. Sorry, did you think it was? You see, in order to get something, you need to give something in return. You want to pick someone's brains about their specialist subject? Then buy them coffee and cake; be respectful of their time; take notes while they're talking, don't be checking your phone for Facebook and Twitter, or texting your best mate "OMG Neil Gaiman is talking to me!" And be prepared to pay for their time: pay the artist, pay the expert, show respect. You're not entitled to help just because you want it.

Consider barter options: perhaps the person whose expertise you're harvesting — Blacksmithing? Sword fighting? Raising giant poodles? – perhaps that person needs assistance with writing or proofreading a promotional brochure or some such. "I propose a trade: an hour of your time for a proofread/edit of your brochure." Once again, it's not all about you — it's mutually beneficial.

5) Pay It Forward

Jeff VanderMeer talks a lot about this, and I guess it's kind of a summary of what I've said above about networking in general. When you get a few steps up the ladder, be sure to remember those who are still in your writing group, people who haven't made it as far along as you. Offer a helping hand when you can because (a) it's good for your karma and (b) it's easier to slide down the ladder than it is to climb it, and at some point in the future your grip may slip. You're going to want the people you helped to remember you kindly. Sow a few favours, do some kindnesses, and they will eventually pay you back.

Suggested Reading

- Jeff VanderMeer's *Booklife: Strategies and Survival Tips for the 21st-Century Writer*
- Cat Rambo's *Creating an Online Presence*
- Angela Slatter's *Online Presence: Pros, Perils and Possibilities* at The Writing Platform

On the Importance of Being Edited (and Editing)

There's a particular kind of arrogance that can trip up a new writer (and sometimes even an experienced one) and it goes something like this, "I just wrote The End, so it's all done."

No.

The End, to paraphrase *The Mummy*'s Imhotep, is just the beginning.

Your first draft is just that: a draft. It needs tender loving care as well as brutal pruning to shape it into a piece that's not only something someone wants to read, but also something that someone (i.e., an editor/publisher) wants to (a) put into print and (b) pay you for.

Editing is a form of auditing. Before an experienced editor/publisher will look at your work, you need to make sure that what you're sending to them is the best you can produce. You must go over your own work to make sure that you have actually written what you think you've written. Are spelling and grammar all present and correct? Does the ending match the beginning? Is the story's internal logic flawless? Do characters act in a manner consistent with their motivation and characterisation? Are those characters believable and engaging, or merely cookie-cutter stereotypes that interest no one? Does the pacing work as it should, or does the story have a flabby middle that needs tightening? Are your descriptions apposite and sharp, rather than simply a bruised purple mess? My expertise is in short stories, but most of what follows can, and should, be applied to longer works as well. I can't cover everything here, but I'll do my best.

The task of self-editing always seems huge, but just like eating an elephant, it should be done one bite at a time. I always start with the small stuff because it's relatively quick and easy and it gives me a sense of achievement that buoys me up to tackle the bigger issues — yes, being a writer is a constant system of sticks and carrots. The basics are always spelling, grammar and punctuation. When you're reading over a draft, put on your critical thought hat: have you used the right word? Have you written 'enervated' when you mean 'energised' because they sound a bit alike? I have marked more student pieces with this kind of assured idiocy in them than I care to remember. Some crackers I cannot burn from my memory include: "She spent the day begatting a meal for her husband," or "This gave the movement the inertia it needed to move forward," and my personal favourite, "she danced around on the stage with a feather Boer around her neck."

Have you used the correct version of words that have different meanings and spellings but sound the same? You're, your, yore? Their, they're, there? Where, we're, wear, were (as in the Old English version meaning 'man')? Flaw, floor, flore (Latin for flowers)? A good idea is to keep a list of words above your desk that you know are a problem for you. Every time you're reading a draft, check against the list, make sure you've got it right. With any luck, the repeated reminders will help embed the correct meanings in your brain. It's easy to make a mistake in the first draft — that's what the first draft is for, making mistakes, throwing the brain-vomit onto the page. What's not forgivable is leaving those mistakes in there after the second or third draft.

Grammatical mistakes, such as disagreement between your

plurals and singulars, most definitely need to be fixed. If you know grammar is not your strong point, then find a writing friend who is good at it and learn from them. Punctuation is also very important: the old saw about "Let's eat Grandma" versus "Let's eat, Grandma" is a perfect illustration as to why punctuation matters. Also collect — and read! — books such as Strunk and White's *The Elements of Style*, Mark Tredinnick's *The Little Green Grammar Book*, or Lynne Truss's most excellent *Eats, Shoots & Leaves*. These reference books should sit beside your dictionary and thesaurus.

And for the love of all that's holy or otherwise, learn how to use apostrophes. Here's *The Oatmeal* to tell you how http://theoatmeal.com/comics/apostrophe.

Another problem to look out for is that of unintentional repetitions. You've described something as 'dark' eighteen times in the space of a page, or seven times in two paragraphs, not because you're going for a considered repetition to build a rhythm or a motif, but because it was the only word you could think of in your rushed first draft. Remember: the thesaurus is your friend. A lot of unintentional repetition occurs in descriptions or actions, so look for them there first. Replace those repeated 'dark's with 'ebony', 'cinereal', 'shadowy', 'murky', 'gunmetal', 'charcoal'. Carefully consider the subtle sense you want the word to convey. There's a whole range of alternatives that will add texture to your writing — but don't go overboard and make a simple sentence read like either an anatomical text or a bad romance novel: "Her heart beat strongly" never, ever needs to be "Her blood-pumping organ palpitated indomitably." Also to note: don't just do a global replacement of the offending word with a new one.

You need to develop an awareness of your crutch words — those you fall back on automatically and don't even think about. Are you a repeat offender with 'seems', 'that', 'suddenly', 'slightly', 'appears', 'maybe'? Do they pepper your manuscript like buckshot? Once again, a reminder list above the desk can work wonders to keep these words from cluttering up your work.

Another thing to consider during the self-edit is the length of your sentences, especially if you're a new writer with less experience in crafting prose. Here's the thing about long sentences: the more words you jam in there, the more likely your reader will get to the end of the sentence and go "Huh? What was the start of that? I've been reading for about fifteen minutes and I forget what the point was." The more words you put between your reader and the story, the more chance your tale has of failing, of losing the reader. There are some writers who are simply masters of the long sentence: Jeff VanderMeer is one of them, Angela Carter is another. They also know this secret: a long sentence set amongst a bunch of shorter, sharper ones will stand out. It will stand out like a jewel; it will make the reader pause, catch their breath, marvel at the craft displayed. Shorter sentences are great for simply transmitting information and action, as well as keeping the pace cracking along. Longer sentences can be where you make your reader think more deeply — but you do need to frame them carefully to their best advantage.

This brings me to Five Dollar Words. Is your narrative crammed with multisyllabic words as a matter of course? Does your sentence look as though it ate a thesaurus? Is said sentence verging on purple, with the prose so ornate and extravagant that it draws attention in the way a lime green mankini does? For the record, that is Bad Attention. The Five Dollar Word is best deployed, like long sentences, in a garden of Five Cent Words. That way it will have more impact.

The idea of minimising purple prose leads to another important characteristic of the short story: brevity. There is an art to making short fiction short and *making it work*. Henry David Thoreau said "Not that the story need be long, but it will take a long while to make it short." This may seem self-evident and you're thinking, "Well, d'uh", but I've critiqued and edited a

LOT of work in which there were too many words for the amount of story contained therein. You don't have the same luxury you've got with a novel, that of great long wandering descriptions: as with life, you don't get a second chance to make a first impression, so do it right the first time. Your descriptions must be powerful but precise: if you're describing a character, give us their outstanding feature/s, the thing/s the reader will remember (or needs to know in order to comprehend the tale). If you're describing a setting, again, tell us what we need to know in order to understand the story, although brevity doesn't mean a white room, i.e. no setting given. It means, as my old friend and mentor Jack Dann says, "What does the camera see?" So, if a television camera were to pan through your scene what would/should it pick up?

What must the reader see when they enter that scene? A shotgun on the mantlepiece? Show us – carefully and casually scattered amongst a few other red herring items – what is going to be essential to the story's resolution. So, if the shotgun is going to be fired by the end of the tale, then show it in the first act, remind us about it (subtly) in the second act, then fire that shotgun in the third. My point? When you're editing/auditing ask yourself "Does my tale do this/work in this way?"

Another important thing to keep in mind is structure. I like a three act structure because it gives you a good guide for where to put which plot points. It's especially useful for new writers to train them in the rhythms of a short story, so they become second nature. When you're editing/auditing your work, ask: do all of the parts make up the whole in the way they need to? Is there too much/not enough set up/foreshadowing in Act One? Is there too much exposition/marking time in Act Two? Is Act Three simply too short or too long? Has the climax of the story occurred in a fashion that leaves the reader saying "Huh?" because the writer hasn't given enough foreshadowing, hints, or breadcrumbs in the previous acts? So, once again, you need to read your draft with a critical gaze: forget that it's your baby and you love it to distraction; actively look for its faults.

Consistency is also critical, not simply in the spelling of particular words, but in the meaning you give to them and the way you use them. For example, if in your story you've allocated a specific meaning of "magical and dangerous" to "weird" and that is a recurring meaning, then keep that word specifically for use in that context. Don't suddenly use it for "a bit off". Similarly, make sure a character's appearance remains consistent – don't change eye or hair colour unless you've also given a very good reason. A one-armed woman should not suddenly be shown using a tool or weapon that requires her to have grown back her other arm, because that says the writer forgot who their character is and the limits within which they must operate. In addition, you must show consistency in a character's motivation and action – don't suddenly have your protagonist acting against their grain *unless* you've given them (and shown the reader) why they are doing so.

Finally, when you've done all of the above, is it over? Can you send it out into the wide world for publication?

No.

You do another draft, a second, a third, a fourth until you can no longer see any problems.

Then can you send it off for publication?

No.

You give it to your writers group or your trusted beta readers and let them find problems with it.

Why? Because, let's face it, we're all certain we know what we've written, and the mind will trick us into seeing words that aren't actually there. You're likely to see the ghost words because you know the story so well, you're used to it, it's like a long-term partner: you've stopped looking properly at their face, you're relying on your memory and you've become too lazy to look for something new. Your beta reader, however, as a person who did not write this thing that means so much to you, is not invested in it – they will see omissions and highlight them. This is an essential part of the critique process, for which you must thicken your skin. You must not be so in love with your story that anyone pointing out its faults causes you to burst into tears/flames/defensive protestations about what you really meant/how no one understands your genius. The whole point of editing is to *make your story the best it can be*. Isn't it better for a beta reader to find these problems rather than the editor/publisher to whom you're hoping to sell it?

The other side of the critiquing coin is that *being* a beta reader for other writers will help you become a better self-editor/auditor. The more you're exposed to the process, the more you'll learn, the more able you'll be to spot issues, and the more all these techniques will become second nature to you. As a matter of courtesy to your beta readers, *always* do a self-edit before you pass your work on because, quite frankly, if all you're doing is writing a really rotten first draft then sending it off for someone else to do the hard work then you're a bad person. No, really, you are.

Now, you're wondering: is it all over? You've self-edited, you've let beta readers gnaw on the entrails of your story-child, you've patched it up, and you've sent this new, beautiful Frankenstein of a thing out into the world. If you're lucky, someone else will love it too, so surely the editing is over. Surely.

No.

Sorry.

An editor/publisher worth their salt will see what's wonderful about your tale, but they'll also see what's been missed. They might have suggestions that will make it even better (sometimes they will have terrible suggestions, too, but that's a subject for another post), and you will find your story is being slashed and stitched yet again.

But that is okay, because you're a professional. You're tough, your skin is thick, and you're wearing your Big Person Pants so you can deal with anything. You are okay with the editing because you want your story to be something that takes a reader's breath away, that stays with them as they go about their day long after they've read the last line. You are okay with the editing because it's all part of the profession. You are okay with the editing because *the whole point of editing is to make your story the best it can be.*

What to Do When You Don't Have a Book Coming Out

OR, WHAT TO EXPECT WHEN YOU'RE NOT EXPECTING

Being a writer may well mean writing all the time (in which case, you're fortunate), or writing in as much of the day or night as you can steal from the world, your family, and your non-writing job. The point is that it's difficult, a lot of effort goes in before anything ever sees the light of day. You're unlikely to be constantly bringing out a new novel, or even a series of short stories. It can be a long time between drinks.

This is about the stuff to do in between times: the useful busywork that will help you keep going. It will help lay the foundations for your next steps. Now, please keep in mind that the usefulness of this advice will vary depending on the point you're at in your career, your degree of self-pity/self-righteousness, and your willingness to drag your butt out of the traditional writerly "nobody loves me, everybody hates me, think I'll go eat worms" impostor syndrome pit.

There's a myth that says once you've got your first book deal, you're set. You'll always have a book deal. That your first publisher will be your forever publisher and you'll be faithful to one another until death do you part. Even then, your literary estate will live on and all those bits of dross you never wanted out in the world will somehow appear in published form as your ghost howls into the void. Wait, where was I going with this?

Oh yes. Your first publisher won't always be your last publisher. You won't necessarily have a novel out every year for the rest of your life. And you know what? This will probably bother you and make you feel bad at some point — or all points, but don't reach for the whiskey and revolver quite yet. There's a good chance (unless you're very well-adjusted — but hey, we're talking about writers here) you will become convinced everyone is going to forget who you are; that you're sliding to the bottom of the snake in life's game of Snakes and Ladders.

You're in between contracts. Your publisher has decided they don't want any more books from you and it's hard not to take that personally. Your books haven't sold as well as they'd wished; your editor has moved on and now you're an orphan; the publishing house is changing direction; their marketing plan of "throwing shit against a wall and seeing what sticks" simply hasn't worked to the surprise of no one but the marketing department. Not to mention that your agent has decided they shall slip away into the night, leaving neither a forwarding address nor even a fiver on the dresser.

It's easy to feel that your career is over.

It's probably not.

There are things you can do:

Keep Writing

Just keep writing. A writer writes, folks. Keep writing. Just coz you're in a slump doesn't mean you've failed. Get off the fainting couch and write. Or, if you insist on staying on the fainting couch, then at least grab a notebook and pen and/or the laptop and keep writing. Because this is the equivalent of stocking up your pantry, so that when someone comes asking for what you've got in your bottom drawer, lo and behold, you will have perhaps 72 manuscripts ready and waiting. Write the next novel because that's your job.

Reprints

Find second and third homes for your previously published short stories. Put in some time researching markets for reprint anthologies, and podcasts that are willing to turn wordery reprints into speakery. And don't forget translation markets that are happy to have reprints for first time translations. See where other people are getting their work reprinted, podcasted and/or translated and see if you can find your way into those venues.

The bonus is that you'll get paid again for something you've already been paid for — huzzah! The rate probably won't be as high, but it's still better than a poke in the eye with a sharp stick. And this can help keep your work circulating during the publishing droughts.

Short Stories

If you've been writing novels, you could try something different and school yourself in the art of the short story — just like a novel only shorter, with fewer characters and probably a more ambiguous ending. Or something like that. That doesn't mean it's easy — it's not, trust me — but it is a way of extending your writing skills and possibly finding new markets and new readership. And even if they don't find a home, you're building up the table of contents for a short story collection somewhere down the track.

Community

One of my personal bugbears are writers who disappear when they haven't got a novel coming out: they only turn up in your feed when there's a book on the way. This is short-sighted and looks very much like you simply can't be bothered interacting unless you've got something to shill. That might not be your intention, however …

There's a community out there of readers and fans who like your work. There's also a community of fellow writers out there who probably understand a lot of what you're going through: talk to them. There are new writers coming up through the ranks who look to those ahead of them for how to act: lead by example. Hint: don't be an asshole.

Stay present in the community. I'm not suggesting that you spend all your time on the socials — coz you should be writing and you might be amazed at how a novel fails to materialise when you're on Facebook — but spend a bit of time interacting with the people you want to read and support, and promote your work when it's coming out. Don't just be that relative who only turns up on the doorstep wanting a handout at Christmas, or because your kid's got Girl Guide cookies to sell (although those are admittedly delicious cookies).

Network

Go to conventions and festivals, even if you're not on panels and don't have a book to promote. Meet people — yes, I know, we really only like people as an abstract concept on our computers where we can block or mute them, but sometimes you need to go out amongst the humans. You might make new friends, have interesting conversations, and form new networks that could be helpful later on to you or someone else in your circle. Or, you know, just enjoy being there and not being "on show".

Go to other people's launches, buy their books, be supportive. Do not, I repeat do NOT advertise on your website that you'll be there. It's not your event! It's not about you. You're not a special guest star unless you're launching the book, and even then, you're just the MC.

If you're in a position to **mentor** a new writer, then do so.

You don't have to give up your time for free (nor should you unless it's your choice), but you can help, and you can influence. You can help shape the future of literature and if that doesn't appeal to your god complex, I don't know what will. You can offer the benefit of your own experience.

Join a **writers' group** — one that suits your needs and the amount of time you're prepared to commit. It can be a safe space to talk out frustrations — writing might be a solitary pursuit, but writers still need some human contact. And your cat, whilst adorable, is probably an asshole (harsh critic), and your dog, also adorable, probably thinks you can do no wrong (rabid fan) — so they are not the best givers of feedback. Also, they can't actually talk. Sorry.

And you know what? These sorts of interactions also give you the chance to learn. There's no point in your career at which you will know everything. Really. I've said it before, and I'll probably say it again: you can always learn something from someone, even if it's that said person is a total butthead. But you learned that, right? Now you have the basis for a new character in a story.

Write Blog Posts

By which I don't mean write anything that could be termed a "manifesto" (and therefore used at your trial), but rather useful posts that can help yourself and others with common experiences and reference points. If you've had an epiphany about your writing process, then write about that — someone else might find that info useful. So might you, at a later date, when you come back to it and think "Hey! That insurmountable problem I'm not surmounting now? I surmounted it before! That's how I did it! Thanks, Past Me."

Don't Sulk

Ultimately, don't skulk. Stay present.

I know it can sometimes feel difficult — and our natural urge towards imposter syndrome is just waiting for the moment to flare up like a nasty rash. The inner critic gets louder and louder.

"I'm irrelevant."

"I have nothing to promote."

"I have nothing coming out."

But those thoughts lose sight of the fact that (a) you probably have had things published and you have already contributed to the literature of the world, and (b) you will probably do so again, if you're not a self-pitying idiot and you continue writing and producing.

How do you keep doing that?

Simple: you do the things above — it's part of the business of writing — and you write for yourself. First and foremost, you are your first audience. If you try to write a first draft of something with the weight of "this must be a bestseller," or "this must win awards", then you are setting yourself up to fail. Write the story you want to write — in order to entertain yourself in the first instance, in order to get the words out of your head. In order to have fun. (OMG look at all those repetitions of "first".)

Your career is unlikely to be a constant stream of hits, accolades, festival circuits — and that's kind of good, because if you're constantly on-the-road, it's hard to write and create. Some people do it, sure. Some people can do it from talent, habit, sheer bloody-minded discipline. I am mostly not one of those people — I'm not good at creating when I'm doing festival-y stuff, when I'm promoting things, because I need a break between tasks that use different parts of my brain. Make the most of the quiet times, because when success hits, it doesn't leave much quiet time. Not a complaint, merely an observation.

Don't waste time envying another person's achievements. What they've got, they worked hard for and their career is just on a different timeline to yours. The only thing you can control is how you react to things. You can either do stuff that is positive and affirming and will help set you up for the next stage (manuscripts in the bottom drawer), or you can throw yourself onto the fainting couch and howl ad infinitum. And still be there when things are looking up (dust bunnies in the bottom drawer).

So, make a list — what are you going to do first?

How Long Does Stuff Take?

And by "stuff" I mean a career as a writer.

To start off, remember this: it's unlikely that the first thing you write — be it short story or novel or article — will be the first thing you publish. I can only talk about my own journey with any authority, so that's what appears below. Also keep in mind: while you can study another writer's career and learn from it, you can't actually replicate it because (a) you're not a Replicator, and (b) the conditions and influences that occurred during their journey aren't going to be the same prevailing winds as for you.

I spent many years scribbling and not sending.

I then spent years scribbling and sending and getting rejections. I used all those rejections (soul-destroying as some were) as fuel, to either learn to write better or — and this one is important — to learn to ignore some opinions. If they weren't helpful, if they didn't make me learn about writing in a positive way, then I learned to ignore them. What they did teach me was that there are people in the writing and publishing community who are assholes, for a whole variety of reasons, but they are assholes nonetheless. I learned (a) not to be like them, and (b) not to engage with them — they've got their own issues that I can't do anything about and don't want to buy into. So, they're not on my radar. Time spent worrying about their opinions is time I have wasted that I could have been using to write.

Then I spent a lot of years scribbling and sending and getting acceptances. And all the time in between I have spent improving my craft. Or trying to at least.

A lot of people seem to think I've been incredibly productive in a short space of time. I'm pretty productive, yes, but I've been doing this for almost 15 years now **with intent**. So, here's a brief timeline to give an idea of how long the "with intent" part of my career has taken. This is my version of "How long does stuff take?"

- 2006: I had my first 2 stories accepted (1 by Shimmer and 1 by Lady Churchill's Rosebud Wristlet). I also published 3 other stories. So, a total of 5 stories.
- 2007: I published 4 stories.
- 2008: I published 8 stories.
- 2009: I published 6 stories.
- 2010: I published 4 new stories (2 co-written with Lisa L. Hannett), 2 collections (one mostly new stories, the other mostly reprints), and 2 reprints.
- 2011: I published 3 new stories, and 2 reprints.
- 2012: I published 3 new stories (2 co-written with Lisa L. Hannett), 1 collection (co-written with Lisa L. Hannett), and 3 reprints.
- 2013: I published 7 new stories (1 co-written with Lisa L. Hannett), and 7 reprints.
- 2014: I published 9 new stories, 3 collections (1 co-written with Lisa L. Hannett; 1 entirely new, 1 mostly new stories, 1 all reprints), and 5 reprints.
- 2015: I published 5 new stories, 1 novella and 11 reprints.
- 2016: I published 7 new stories, 2 collections (both mostly reprints), 1 novel and 3 reprints.

- 2017: I published 9 new stories, 1 novel and 9 reprints.
- 2018: I published 5 new stories, 1 novel, and 10 reprints.
- 2019: I published 5 new stories and 7 reprints.
- 2020: I published 5 new stories, 1 collection (mostly reprints), 1 collection that's a re-release, 1 collection of microfiction, and 3 reprints.
- 2021: I published six new stories, 1 novel (All the Murmuring Bones), a collection of short stories (by mid-2021 there will be enough reprints for another collection and I'll write two or three new shorts to go with that), and 4 reprint stories, and two translations.
- 2022: If the world doesn't end, I will publish 1 novel (*The Path of Thorns*), this new chapbook, a new reprint collection, four or five new short stories, several other reprint projects, and an illustrated book.

So, you can see how many of those collections are mostly reprints — stories pulled together from several years before to sit with other newer ones and freshly written ones. Hopefully they all fit nicely.

In there are also some award nominations and some wins (two of those for works co-written with Lisa L. Hannett).

There are definitely more nominations than wins. Now, if I never win another award, I am perfectly okay with that because what I got from these awards, apart from the joy of some very nice trophies and the buzz of accepting awards whilst wearing no shoes, was attention from publishers and readers overseas. I was able to expand my reading audience, and it led to new publishing contracts and a bunch of translations (into Bulgarian, Chinese, Russian, Italian, Spanish, Japanese, Polish, French and Romanian).

- 2020 Aurealis Award for Best Collection
- 2020 Australian Shadows Award for Best Collection

- 2017 Australian Shadows Award for Best Novel
- 2016 Aurealis Award for Best Collection
- 2015 Ditmar Award for Best Novella
- 2014 World Fantasy Award for Best Collections
- 2014 Aurealis Award for Best Collection
- 2014 Aurealis Award for Best Horror Short Story
- 2014 Aurealis Award for Best Fantasy Short Story
- 2012 British Fantasy Award for Best Short Story
- 2010 Aurealis Award for Best Collection
- 2010 Aurealis Award Best Fantasy Short Story

What you don't see from these lists — but should be able to extrapolate — is the amount of work done over a very long period of time. Consistent writing and polishing and submitting. Researching markets, attending cons, networking either for myself or others. All. The. Time.

If I didn't love writing so much, I'd call it grinding until I got my XP up. My point is that this career is *cumulative*. It doesn't happen overnight.

You're basically a duck: moving elegantly on the surface of a pond, while beneath you're paddling like mad. Many's the day when I've felt like a duck with its ballast incorrectly weighted, my head underwater, my feet in the air, very un-elegant and drowning. But I've kept going. I've learned from those further up the ladder, and I've done my best to help those lower down.

And I have kept moving.

And writing.

Because, in the end, everything adds up.

Finding an Agent: the Ugly Truth

This article originally appeared in The Australian Writer's Marketplace 2011/12, now updated based on a further eight-ish years of experiences, good and bad. Many thanks to Dennan Chew and Ron Serdiuk for their wise comments.

Literary agents manage, in theory, all the business of a writer's work. This includes submissions, sales, contracting, publication, translation, production and reproduction. They act as a conduit between authors and publishers (and sometimes editors). If a writer's lucky, their agent is a proactive sword and shield, utterly loyal to their client's interests (no pressure) … wait, that kind of makes them sound like feudal knights with a Lord or a Pope to answer to unquestioningly … so scratch that. Your agent is hopefully an intelligent, independent professional with your career's best interests at heart. Yeah, let's go with that.

They use their industry knowledge and contacts to sell projects to book publishers, or television and film producers, sometimes bring business to your door, act as a gatekeeper, and generally negotiate contracts for you to the best of their ability and professional competence.

They sound fabulous, don't they? Would you like one? Who wouldn't?

Well, unfortunately while it is a truth universally acknowledged, that a writer in possession of a good manuscript, must be in want of a literary agent, it is a fact less universally recognised that agents are a very difficult commodity to acquire. In Australia, there is a rather small number of working literary agents and a very large number of wannabe writers. The pool of agents does not seem to be growing, at least not at speed — possibly because, like pandas, they don't breed in captivity — while the number of writers vying for attention is most certainly on the rise. Or perhaps (more reasonably), it's because we have a smaller marketplace, smaller print runs, a smaller book-buying public, so the system does not lend itself to a growth in the agent population as the ecosystem can't provide all of them with a decent living.

So, How Do You Get An Agent?

I always say that you need to be an informed writer: learn about all aspects of the business (writing, publishing, editing, marketing, sales, etc) because your job doesn't end when you write "The End". Be informed, so that you will sense something is wrong when someone tries to sell you a delightful piece of swampland or the Sydney Harbour Bridge. Join your local writers' centre and go to their industry evenings; go to the business of writing panels at festivals; listen and learn. Your bullshit detector will be far more highly calibrated if you are an informed writer.

So, having become informed, put your best submission foot forward. Always remember that you are, until you become a mega-super-rich bestseller, the supplicant. You may well have an awesome product — your book — but no one knows that until they actually read it. Therefore, how do you get an agent to do that all-important action, the "looking at of the book"? Here are the highlights:

1. **Research your target**, but not in a stalking kind of way. I mean establish which agents represent your genre because there's no point in sending a bodice-ripping romance to someone who only represents espionage thrillers with explosions on every second page. Make sure you check and follow their submission guidelines to the letter; it's not like the Pirates' Code, you don't get to pick and choose which bits you follow and which you don't. Make sure you peruse their list of clients carefully. Do you recognise any of the names? Do the covers of those clients' books look professionally produced? Do you know an existing client well enough to ask them about how they find their agent; are they happy together? Also, if you are writing very much like someone already on the existing list, why would they take you on? Can you offer something new? If not, then move on.
2. **Write first, agent second**. By this I mean do not approach an agent before you've written anything. You'd be wasting their time and yours. You are meant to be presenting them with a product they can sell in order to (hopefully) make both of you an income. For one cannot buy groceries with artistic integrity. Cafés take a very dim view of trying to swap a sonnet for smashed avocado on toast and a chai latte. Agents run a business: you and your book(s) are their stock-in-trade. No book = nothing to talk about.[1]
3. **Be polite** to everyone. Always. In life, and in writing and publishing. Agents talk to each other; they talk to publishers, editors, other writers, booksellers, marketing and sales people. If you get a reputation as someone who is unprofessional and unpleasant to deal with, the whole industry will eventually know. Similarly, if you're creating an online platform, remember that someone is always watching/reading

and search engines will find anything you've ever put into e-space, so be wary. If you're rude and complaining about someone, it can and will come back to haunt you.

4. **Write a cover letter** that will get attention; make it succinct and relevant. A five page epistle will not help your cause. Introduce yourself in the first short paragraph, including any writing credits, awards or courses you may have done. If you have a particular area of expertise or experience in the subject you're writing about, then say so: "As I was the captain of a pirate ship for fifteen years, I am eminently qualified to write a novel about a pirate captain." The next paragraph should be about your novel: specify genre, length, target audience and a summary of the plot (a 'blurb') in one, two or three sentences — any further detail should be left for the synopsis. In the next paragraph, you may like to mention what inspired you to write the book, and note any authors whose work is similar to yours. As a courtesy, if you're simultaneously submitting to other agents/publishers, mention that as well. Make sure you address your letter to the right person and do not, repeat, do not, write "Dear Sir" when the recipient is female — or indeed, vice versa. If someone has a title, like "Dr", then use it. Do not be over-familiar with someone you do not know; or indeed with someone you do.

5. **Be able to summarise your novel in** (a) a grab line, (b) a blurb (25 words or less), AND (c) a one to two page synopsis. If you cannot be succinct about the plot of your novel, you cannot grab someone's attention. Think of it like this: you have a 60 second elevator ride with an agent and you need to tell them about your novel. A rambling ode will not cut it. Do not,

repeat, do not hit the emergency stop button to gain more time.

6. **And remember this:** just because one agent says no, it doesn't mean no agent will ever want to represent you. Another agent may well love your work, so you cannot take rejection personally.[2] Persist.[3] Behave like a professional, because you should be dealing with professionals. Listen to the advice you are given, even when (or perhaps *especially* when) it's from someone rejecting your manuscript because just maybe they are right, and you can learn something new.

Things Not to Do

1. Don't call an agent and demand that they take you on. Don't tell them they'd be lucky to have you, and that they should really get onboard now! And yes, I know I already said this in a footnote, but I really, *really* mean it. Should you, for some reason best known to you and the god of your choosing, decide to use a phone for its original and archaic purpose, i.e., phoning someone, then do not, for the love of all that's holy, be rude to the receptionist. Do not then demand to speak to their boss, the *real* agent. You know what? Sometimes the person answering the phone *is* the agent, not a lackey — so, once again, be polite to everyone. Plus, sometimes the agent will ask the receptionist what they thought of the person on the other end of the phone; so keep that in mind before you get snippy with the help.
2. In case of meeting an actual honest-to-goodness agent at a writers' festival/cocktail party, etc, don't thrust a manuscript under their nose or into their handbag or under the toilet door. It may seem like an opportunity, but it's **not**. You can mention politely that you're a

writer, and *if* they ask if you've got a manuscript and what it's about, then feel free to give the blurb (elevator pitch). If the agent is interested, they *might* ask to see said manuscript. They might even give you a business card. Also, they might not, and if they don't then take the hint; do not insist. Please do not spend the entire function monopolising the agent. I know it's exciting, a real live agent and not a blow-up one, however, they might want to talk to someone else, they might have friends there, or they might just want some quiet time hiding on a balcony, drinking the festival's horrible wine and having a sneaky cigarette before the fire alarm goes off.

3. Do not send gifts (or put glitter in envelopes, as there's a special Hell reserved for people who do that). They will not work. They count as forms of bribery, graft and corruption. You're not an international arms dealer trying to make time with a Prime Minister, President or Secretary for Defence. You're not trying to win favour with a difficult child. Just don't.

4. If the agent's website says you will pay a reading fee to get them to look at your manuscript, then quietly walk away. Better yet, run screaming and tell all the other writers you can find about this. An agent makes their money from the commission they take on the book deal they negotiate for you. Part of your agent research should be to check out sites like Preditors & Editors and Writer Beware (go on, do the Google) — there is a lot of info out there in Internetland that can be useful to an informed writer.

5. Be aware that there's a bit of a Catch-22 with the "Do I approach an agent or a publisher first" question. You can approach publishers directly yourself (a lot have open submission periods once a week), but keep in mind that if you've already approached and been

rejected by most of the publishers in Australia, then an agent cannot do much for you with a book that's already been rejected (unless it's had significant reworking and the agent can vouch for its improved condition).

6. Don't ring after two weeks demanding to know why the agent hasn't contacted you. You may have to wait for months — deal with it. They will probably have a note on their website telling you what the average response period is. Put a note in your diary; if you've not heard back by then, then send a polite enquiry via email. If you've not heard back by the end of a month (like a proper four-week month), then feel free to send another polite email which thanks them for their kind consideration, but you are withdrawing the submission and sending it elsewhere. That's all you need (indeed should) do; no fanfare, no huffing and puffing, no dramatic exiting stage left whilst trailing black veils behind you and shouting, "I said Good Day, sir!".[4] This is not a calculated kick to the ego, it is not personal insult: just move on and do the productive, professional activities that progress your career.

Do You Need an Agent?

Opinions on the importance of agents vary, even (or especially) amongst established authors (possibly because if you've already got one, you can afford to feel a bit jaded, or take things for granted). If you've been around long enough, published enough books, gone to enough conventions, been mostly polite and professional, you will probably find you know a lot of editors and publishers well enough to not only drink whiskey with them in convention hotel bars, but also to go to their homes and not be escorted out by the constabulary while someone shouts, "The terms of the restraining order were very clear!" You can send them emails and Christmas cards, or even *gasp* call them on the phone.

If you get to this point in your career, you might also be in a position where you don't need an agent to pitch your next book to a publisher ... you can do that yourself over a beverage. Having gained a publisher's attention in a fashion that won't lead to incarceration, some writers will then either negotiate contracts for themselves, or hand the next stage of the process over to their agent.

Some agents do everything for you; some agents only do the bits you don't want to/are not sufficiently expert at doing. Some agents don't do even the minimal things they should or have agreed to do in their agreement with you (more on that below).

My point is this: what *you* think an agent is going to do for you and what *they* think they are going to do for you might well be two different things. Some literary agencies call themselves "full service agencies" — which makes me giggle because I am basically a teenage boy — but it actually means that they manage all aspects of your career. **But** just make sure (a) you're both clear on what those aspects are and (b) they do what they say they're going to do. You will, as an informed writer, have a written and signed agreement with your agent (no handshakes, no gentlefolks' agreements, only WRITTEN, SIGNED, HARD COPIES KEPT IN YOUR FILING CABINET), which you will have read, understanding the print whether it be fine, gross or pleasingly plump. If you have not understood any part of your agreement, ask until you have an answer you understand and with which you concur. The agreement should set out things like the commission your agent earns, the services they will undertake for you, and a termination clause in case you part ways.

Some agents will look over your contract and advise on it for a fee without actually being your agent. If you don't need an agent to agent for you, but you do need someone with specialised publishing contract knowledge, then this is the person for you. Like a Tinder date: some benefits, no real commitment.

Breaking Up Is Hard to Do

So, what if you've got an agent but you're not happy with them? Now, this bit is hard, especially when you've taken so long to actually find an agent. You thought they would be your forever agent, but for one reason or another, things are not working out. Whether someone is failing to put the cap back on the literary toothpaste, refusing to put the toilet seat down in the dark of night whilst also failing to change the toilet roll, things are going south. Deals are not being made, contracts are falling through, terms are not what they promised, emails are not being answered, no one has time to discuss a strategy for moving forward. This is a relationship like any other. For a while, you hang on. You tell yourself, "It's still good! We can work through it. I can compromise!"

Until one day, you just can't. Your nerves are frayed, you're grumpy all the time, you're not getting answers and your needs are not getting met. You really don't want to say, "We need to talk," because you know that is the end of all relationships. Also, OMG you will then be AGENTLESS. *cue horrified screams* But here's the thing: if the required work is not getting done, if you are stressed by the situation and nothing is being done to remedy the problem, if you and your agent are at odds and your differences are irreconcilable, then there is no point having this particular agent. You are wasting each other's time and moving closer to a frustration-induced axe-murder scenario.

Having no agent is better than having a bad agent. Having no relationship is better than having a bad relationship.

Also keep in mind that maybe you were not the easiest client. Maybe you weren't what they thought they were getting either. Maybe they lost faith in your writing, just like you lost faith in their agenting. Also, you are not going to be their only client, so you need to be patient and remember that you are not the centre of the universe. Sometimes this is difficult, because as writers we spend a lot of time alone, and it makes us selfish and inward-looking with a tendency towards talking more to imaginary friends than actual ones. But still, learn to know when it's time to move on (from all relationships, quite frankly).

Cut your losses and leave, then start again. Be polite. Write a polite break-up letter. Be professional. Don't sledge the old agent in public. Remember: private fainting couch tantrum, public professional behaviour.

But Do Break Up

Habit is easy even when it's injurious to us in some way, shape or form. Change is hard and it's difficult to remember to do the different new thing instead of the habitual old thing. But only for a while. And a bad agent who's not doing what they've agreed to do? They are not helping your cause or career. If they're not actively hindering, then the very least they are doing is keeping you in stasis, and there's no progress in stasis. Quite frankly, the only good time to be in stasis is when you're on a generation ship going to a new world many light years away, or being kept alive until they can find a cure for your terrible disease and/or upload your consciousness into a sexy robot body.

Remember this also: your agency agreement might specify a period during which you cannot sign with another agent — you need to observe this. Also be aware that an agent will continue to receive commission on future royalties from books for which they negotiated the deals.

In Conclusion

Ultimately, chances are that no one will manage your career in precisely the way you want them to, but if you make a point of setting expectations from the outset, then you have a baseline to point to later on if things go off the rails. Key performance indicators can help in all aspects of life (or make it miserable, too). You need to have that conversation about expectations and perceptions: if you don't tell someone what you want, then they won't know, and they probably don't read minds. The corollary is this: if you *do* tell someone what you want and they are not willing to do it, and they repeatedly fail to deliver (especially when they say they *will* deliver), then it is time to consider your options. Otherwise, as with all relationships, the choice is remaining in a situation that just makes you unhappy and unsatisfied. And nobody wants that. Always have an escape plan; it's what an informed writer would do.

So, that problem with a lack of Australian agents? How about an overseas agent? Follow the same steps as listed in this mind-numbingly long article, but be aware of the 'portability' of your work. By that I mean, will your writing appeal to an overseas market? Will it be relevant and saleable in another locale? If not, then chances are an overseas agent won't look at your work. Don't self-reject, but do be aware of the possibility that the writing might not appeal elsewhere — **but** there are a lot of other markets, so persist.

An agent should have good contacts in the writing and publishing industry and a thorough knowledge of current industry trends and developments. They should know about copyright, contracts, overseas rights, subsidiary rights, and other legal issues related to the sale of intellectual properties inside out. They should have contacts with agents in other countries just in case you're lucky enough to sell foreign rights. They should be the sort of person you want to conduct your business for you. They don't need to be your friend, but you do need to feel you can trust them.

You don't *need* an agent, but they can be an invaluable part of your business team (and writing is a business). The agent is like the Kelly Bag of the literary world — nice to have but sometimes

Finding an Agent: the Ugly Truth

you have to do without. But you can increase your chances of getting one (and hopefully a good one) if you follow the advice above.

---

1. Just because you've finished the first draft does not mean it's time to query: make sure you've revised and edited, had outside eyes on the manuscript, and polished the thing until it shines BEFORE you query. Do not, repeat, do not send your first draft.
2. Caveat the First: unless the rejection includes the words "This is the worst spelled, most grammatically incorrect manuscript I've ever seen, with unspeakable subject matter, and it was written in crayon" ... then you might need to reconsider your life choices.
3. Caveat the Second: although do remember that if an agent rejects you, don't argue and try to convince them you'd be great together. If you hear the words, "Baby, I can change!" issue forth from your lips, just stop. Very bad tactic in all facets of life.
4. Don't get me wrong: I love a good fit of histrionics. I can and will throw myself onto the fainting couch and wail BUT I do this in the privacy of my own home with only the dogs and housemates as witnesses.

Thank you

Thank you to those folk who've done early reads of these posts over the years: Ron Serdiuk, Dennan Chew, Lisa L. Hannett, Angie Rega, Suzanne J. Willis, Kathleen Jennings, and Kylie Thompson, and to Peter M. Ball and Brain Jar Press for ideas so crazy they just might work.

About the Author

Angela Slatter is the author of the gothic fantasy novels *All the Murmuring Bones* and the forthcoming *The Path of Thorns* (Titan Books), and the supernatural crime novels *Vigil*, *Corpselight* and *Restoration* (Jo Fletcher Books). She's also written eleven short story collections, including *The Girl with No Hands and Other Tales*, *Sourdough and Other Stories*, *The Bitterwood Bible and Other Recountings*, and *A Feast of Sorrows: Stories*, and the novellas, *Of Sorrow and Such* and *Ripper*.

Vigil was nominated for the Dublin Literary Award in 2018, and Angela has won a World Fantasy Award, a British Fantasy

Award, a Ditmar, two Australian Shadows Award and seven Aurealis Awards. *All the Murmuring Bones* was shortlisted for the Queensland Premier's Literary Awards' Book of the Year in 2021. Angela's short stories have appeared in Australian, UK and US *Best Of* anthologies such *The Mammoth Book of New Horror, The Year's Best Dark Fantasy and Horror, The Best Horrorof the Year, The Year's Best Australian Fantasy and Horror, and The Year's Best YA Speculative Fiction*. Her work has been translated into Bulgarian, Chinese, Russian, Italian, Spanish, Japanese, Polish, Hungarian, Turkish, French and Romanian. Film rights have been optioned for her novelette "Finnegan's Field".

She has an MA and a PhD in Creative Writing, is a graduate of Clarion South 2009 and the Tin House Summer Writers Workshop 2006, and in 2013 she was awarded one of the inaugural Queensland Writers Fellowships. In 2016 Angela was the Established Writer-in-

Residence at the Katharine Susannah Prichard Writers Centre in Perth. She has been awarded career development funding by Arts Queensland, the Copyright Agency and the Australia Council for the Arts.

Find her online at www.angelaslatter.com

- facebook.com/angelaslatterauthor
- twitter.com/AngelaSlatter
- instagram.com/angelaslatter
- amazon.com/Angela-Slatter/e/B005QQ9FOA

Also by Angela Slatter

You Are Not Your Writing features Angela Slatter's best advice on managing social media, understanding the role awards play in your developing career, the hierarchy of rejection, and strategically building your career and network of other writers. Most importantly, they draw the line between the writer and their work, and illustrate the dangers of mistaking one for the other.

Whether you're a new writer seeking advice on taking the next step, or a fan of Slatter's fiction looking for a glimpse behind the scenes, this chapbook is a peek into the mindset and philosophy of one of Australia's most acclaimed writers of fantasy and horror.

Find out more at www.brainjarpress.com

Angela Slatter's Fiction

Sourdough Stories

Sourdough & Other Stories
The Bitterwood Bible & Other Recountings
The Tallow Wife & Other Stories
Of Sorrow & Such
All the Murmuring Bones as *A.G. Slatter*
The Path of Thorns as *A.G. Slatter* (Forthcoming)
The Bone Lantern (Forthcoming)

Collections

The Girl With No Hands & Other Tales
Midnight & Moonshine (with Lisa L. Hannett)
The Female Factory (with Lisa L. Hannett)
Black Winged Angels
Winter Children & Other Chilling Tales
A Feast Of Sorrows: Stories
The Heart Is a Mirror For Sinners & Other Stories
Red New Day & Other Micro-fictions
The Wrong Girl and Other Warnings (Forthcoming)

Verity Fassbinder

Vigil
Corpselight
Restoration

Thank You For Buying This Brain Jar Press Chapbook

To receive special offers, bonus content, and info on new releases and other great reads, visit us online at www.BrainJarPress.com

www.ingramcontent.com/pod-product-compliance
Lightning Source LLC
Chambersburg PA
CBHW021452080526
44588CB00009B/809